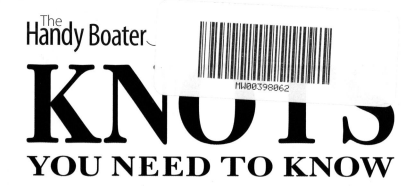

The
Handy Boater

KNOTS
YOU NEED TO KNOW

Easy-to-Follow Guide to the 30 Most Useful Knots

The Handy Boater

KNOTS
YOU NEED TO KNOW

Easy-to-Follow Guide to the 30 Most Useful Knots

skills institute
press

Distributed By
Fox Chapel Publishing

FOX CHAPEL
PUBLISHING

© 2011 by Skills Institute Press LLC
"The Handy Boater" series trademark of Skills Institute Press
Published and distributed in North America by Fox Chapel Publishing Company, Inc.,
East Petersburg, PA.

Knots You Need to Know is an original work, first published in 2011.

Portions of text and art previously published by and reproduced under license with
Direct Holdings Americas Inc.

ISBN 978-1-56523-589-2

Library of Congress Cataloging-in-Publication Data

Knots you need to know.
    p. cm. -- (The handy boater)
Includes index.
ISBN 978-1-56523-589-2 (alk. paper)
1. Knots and splices--Handbooks, manuals, etc.
VM533.K66 2011
623.88'82--dc22
                            2011007650

To learn more about the other great books from Fox Chapel Publishing,
or to find a retailer near you, call toll-free 800-457-9112 or visit us at
www.FoxChapelPublishing.com.

Printed in Singapore
Second printing

Contents

WHAT YOU WILL LEARN

Chapter 1
Knowing the Ropes, page 10
Choosing the appropriate rope
for the job is just as important as
choosing the knot to tie it with.

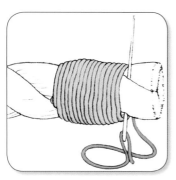

Chapter 2
Tight Finishes, page 14
Whether whipping or seizing,
finishing off a rope end will keep
it from unraveling.

Chapter 3
The Knots to Know, page 18
In choosing the right knot to use,
the boater should be guided by
the purpose needed.

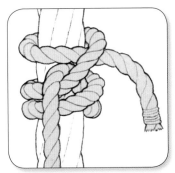

Chapter 4

Tying to Lines and Rings, page 48
Boaters need to know how to
secure lines to other lines and
to rings.

Chapter 5

Splicing, page 58
The best way to make a permanent
loop in a line is to make an
eye splice.

Chapter 6

Additional Uses, page 76
A solid knowledge of knots will
allow a boater to make ladders
and lanyards as well.

INTRODUCTION

Ropework:
Plain and Fancy

Beyond the 10 or so basic knots, splices, bends, and hitches that every boatman must know, there are an almost infinite number of additional rope forms, decorative and utilitarian, which can be mastered to improve both the beauty and function of his vessel. The multiple half hitches being bent onto a steering wheel, for example, appear to be designed just for decoration; actually, they serve the eminently practical function of giving the skipper a firm grip on the helm. The Portuguese bowline was designed long ago for straightforward utility, yet like all of the other ropework shown on subsequent pages, it has a handsome and seamanly look to it (pages 28–29). In addition to the useful and aesthetic virtues of these knots, the tying of them is itself a satisfying pastime, a kind of maritime sculpture that quickly takes form under the hands and eyes of the boatman. That is one reason why sailors since ancient times have occupied themselves with this practice; the crews of sailing ships used to while away the long sea voyages by trying to outdo one another in knotsmanship.

All these knots have a long history. In fact, some have outlived their initial purpose and survive today in an entirely new guise. The tack knot (pages 44–45), for instance, was once used on windjammers to secure the tack, or forward edge, of a sail. Today, though, metal fittings have taken over the function of securing the tack; but the tack knot is still being tied—usually as a decorative fillip for the end of a bell rope or grab line. One old seaman's yarn tells of an English tar named Matthew Walker who was condemned to death, then offered a pardon on condition that he tie a knot that the judge—himself a former seaman—would not be able to undo. The sailor disappeared into his cell with 10 fathoms of rope and devised, exactly in the middle of the line, the deceptive knot that today bears his name. He then reemerged to present his invention to the judge. The judge was stumped, and Matthew Walker received his pardon as promised.

This story conveys a number of enduring truths about knots. One is that in the sailor's world, a knot exists for every conceivable purpose—including saving the life of a condemned man. Another is that the vast majority of knots in the nautical spectrum, though they may at first appear incomprehensible even to a fairly well educated eye, are easy and relatively quick to tie once the boater learns how. The knot that confounded the judge, for example, can be fashioned within about two minutes—though nowadays it is generally made near the end of a line rather than in the middle—by anyone who knows the trick *(pages 46–47)* of unlaying the strands before he starts. Several of the other knots on these pages are, like the Matthew Walker, started by unlaying the line and reworking the separate strands. Others, among them the intricate-looking monkey's fist *(pages 32–35)*, are tied with the end of the line remaining intact.

Different kinds of rope have special qualities that suit them to certain kinds of knots. The easiest material to use is cotton; it can be manipulated comfortably—without chafing fingertips or splitting nails, which prickly manila has a tendency to do—and it serves well for knife lanyards and ditty bags. However, cotton is neither strong nor durable and should never be used for working lines. For heavy-duty apparatus, such as sheets, halyards, anchor lines, or a water-ski rig, modern synthetics such as nylon and Dacron are best; they neither shrink nor rot after having been soaked in water. And for good, workaday versatility, many boatmen feel that nothing beats manila; it makes a sturdy knot whose sculptural outlines clearly show, and has an old-fashioned look that warms the hearts of tradition-minded seamen.

CHAPTER 1:
Knowing the Ropes

Rope is the seaman's most essential tool. It tethers every vessel to a dock or mooring, or secures it to an anchor. For the man in a sailboat, ropes are, in addition, the reins that harness the wind in his sails.

The flexibility and strength of rope are astonishing. It can be made into knots, bends and splices; it coils neatly for stowing; and yet an ordinary manila rope thinner than a man's little finger can carry a load of hundreds of pounds.

The reason for the pliancy and holding power of rope lies in its construction. The basic structural element in virtually all rope is a collection of threadlike fibers that are twisted together into thicker components called yarns. These yarns, in turn, are twisted into strands; and the strands are either laid up (i.e., twisted once again) or else braided together, as shown on page 12, to form the finished rope.

In the past, rope fibers were made from natural materials such as bark, grasses, or leaves—and some still are. Hemp, manila, cotton, and linen rope still find favor on many modern boats. However, all natural fibers tend to rot, and most boatmen have turned to longer-lived synthetics such as nylon and Dacron.

Not only are synthetics immune to rot and mildew, but they are also considerably stronger than natural materials. Both nylon and Dacron will carry more than twice the load of a manila line of equal size. Nylon rope, furthermore, will stretch up to 20 percent of its length, making it useful for docking and anchoring lines, which require elasticity (pages 90–93). Dacron, on the other hand, stretches very little, so it is ideal for running rigging, which holds sails tautly in place.

Both nylon and Dacron have another inherent advantage. They are smoother and even more pliable than natural fibers. Hence, the synthetics can readily be made up into braided line. And a braided line shows far less tendency to snarl than does a line laid up in twists.

The strongest and most long-lasting of all rope is made of steel wire, commonly used aboard powerboats for their vital steering cables, and on sailboats for such maximum-stress rigging as shrouds and stays. Halyards, too, are generally wire, at least along some of their length: their standing parts are of steel to take the heaviest strain, while the tail ends are of Dacron for easy handling.

The Right Rope for the Right Job

anchor rodes	nylon
docking lines	nylon manila
towlines	nylon manila
shrouds and stays	wire manila Dacron (prestretched)
sheets	Dacron manila linen wire (with rope tail)
halyards	wire Dacron (prestretched) manila linen
steering cables	wire
life lines	Dacron wire (plastic-coated)
fender lines	Dacron manila cotton linen
centerboard pennants sail boltropes	wire Dacron
flag halyards	cotton linen manila Dacron
whipping and seizing	hemp (oiled) linen nylon (waxed) manila (oiled) cotton (oiled)

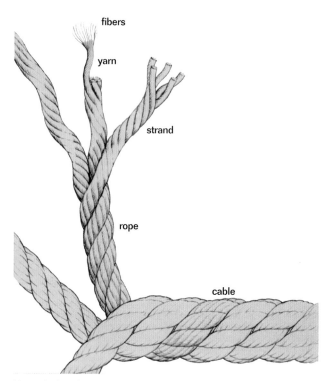

fibers

yarn

strand

rope

cable

Unraveled to show its anatomy, a typical rope is built up from fibers twisted in a counterclockwise direction or into so-called right-handed yarns. The yarns, in turn, are formed into strands, and the strands laid up into rope. The direction of the twist reverses at each step so that the last twist conventionally is a right-handed one.

In a completed rope the strands are twined diagonally to the rope's length, but the yarns within each strand lie parallel. The ultimate in fiber construction, the cable-laid rope *(above)* is formed from three ropes twisted together. Used for docking lines on large ships, the cable has greater elasticity than standard rope of equal diameter.

Plaited rope is formed from pairs of strands that are intertwined like a child's pigtail. Popular for sheets on sailboats, plaited rope has a knobby surface, making it easier to grip. And because it has no diagonal lay, it is not subject to a twisted rope's tendency to curl up on itself in kinks.

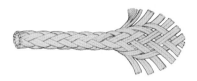

Single braided rope *(left)* is interwined like plaited rope *(above)*, but with more strands and a smoother, more uniform exterior. In this example, 24 strands are braided together in pairs. Though useful for spinnaker sheets, single braided rope is hollow in the center and flattens under tension—a trait that may cause it to bind in a block or on a winch.

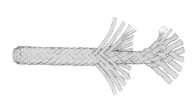

Double-braided rope, a favorite for sheets, is made up of two single-braided synthetic ropes, one inside for a core and a second outside for a cover. This combination produces maximum strength and minimum stretch. Core and cover can share the load; or a sturdier core may carry the load, while a cover protects the core from abrasion.

Wire rope, like twisted rope, has left-laid strands twisted into right-laid rope. Wire rope may be hollow; or it may incorporate a single straight wire as a core, or an oil-saturated hemp core that lubricates the rope against rust. Manufacturers identify wire rope by the number of wires per strands and strands per rope; the example at left is a 7 by 7.

CHAPTER 2:
Tight Finishes

All rope ends need to be finished off to keep them from raveling. Binding up the ends—a process called whipping *(below and right)*—secures the ends of most lines. With synthetic rope, which unlays more easily than does natural fiber, the ends should first be taped and then fused with heat *(below)* before whipping.

When doubling a rope around a thimble to form a permanent eye, the end should be secured with a tight binding called a seizing *(page 16)*. Wire is normally finished *(page 17)* with a terminal fitting attached by machine—though a homemade job can be done with small fittings called bulldog clips.

Techniques for Whipping

Waterproof rigger's tape, wrapped tightly around a rope against the lay *(near right)*, keeps the strands from unraveling until a permanent whipping can be bound on. When a new length of rope is cut from a coil, apply tape on both sides of the point to be cut before the rope is severed. Taping the slippery ends of synthetic rope makes fusing and whipping easier. For fusing *(far right)*, the best tool is an electrically heated knife used by riggers; but the job can be done with a soldering iron or the flame from a match. To make a solid, blunt end, apply heat around the edges and work toward the center.

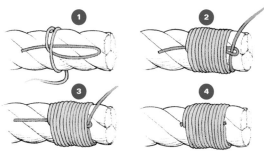

A common whipping permanently secures loose strands at the end of a rope without the use of tools. With marline or whipping twine, make a narrow loop about a half inch longer than the rope's diameter (1) and lay it lengthwise along the rope. Bind the twine tightly over the loop with turns taken against the lay of the rope, working toward the end. When the length of the whipping equals the diameter of the rope, slip the working end of the twine through the loop (2). Pull the free end of the twine (3) so that the loop carries the working end snugly under the turns. Clip off both ends close to the turns (4).

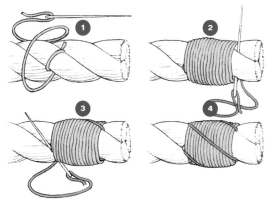

Palm-and-needle whipping makes the neatest work, but requires a sailmaker's needle and a leather palm to drive the needle through the rope. First anchor a length of waxed sail twine with a few stitches around a strand (1). Wrap the twine tightly around the rope against the lay, working toward the end. When the whip is as long as the rope's diameter (2), pass the needle under a strand so it emerges in the next groove between strands. Bring the twine back along the groove and stitch it under the next strand (3). Repeat until all grooves are filled. Then stitch the end of the twine through a strand and clip the end (4).

Seizing for a Thimble

A chafeproof metal fitting called a thimble, seized into a rope end, forms a useful terminal. First make an eye in some twine by tucking the end through a few of its own strands. Then make a noose around the two rope parts by passing the end of the twine through its eye (1). Working toward the thimble, make 12 turns (2), and tuck the end under the last turn. Add a second layer of 11 so-called riding turns, working back toward the eye in the twine. Pass the end through the eye, slip it between the rope parts (3) and make a few crossing turns around the riding turns. Finish with a half hitch (4).

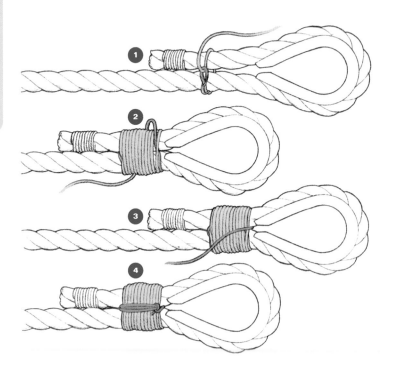

Eyes for Wire-Rope Ends

Wire terminals typically consist of eyed metal sheaths, called swages (1), which are fused around the wire's end under great heat and pressure by a special machine in a supplier's shop. Alternately, crimp-type fittings (2) may be put on either by a supplier or in a home workshop. The wire is folded back on itself and held in place by a soft metal sleeve, which is pressed around the wire by a vise. Temporary shipboard fastenings can be made with bulldog clips (3), U-shaped clips that slip over both pieces of wire and are bolted into a plate that grips them securely.

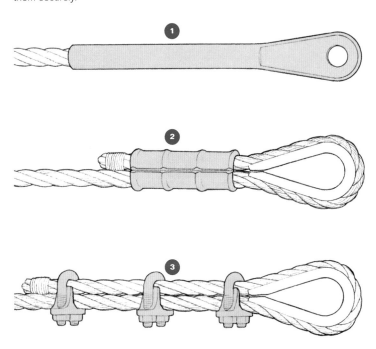

CHAPTER 3:
The Knots to Know

Of all the necessary nautical skills, perhaps none is as mystifying to the novice as the tying of ropes. An almost infinite number of configurations can be made in rope, and over the course of nautical history perhaps 2,000 of these have come into some kind of functional or decorative use. Yet a practical seaman can get along comfortably and safely for a lifetime by mastering only the nine basic knots and the splice shown at right.

In everyday usage most people—sailors included—refer to any interlacing of one or more pieces of rope as a knot. In its more precise nautical meaning, however, a knot is formed only when a rope is turned back and tied on itself—as in the top row on page 20. The fastening together of two rope ends to extend the length of line is called, technically, a bend, e.g., the double sheet bend. A configuration of rope tied around an object—which can be another rope—is a hitch (*page 20*). And an interweaving of one set of rope strands with another, to secure together two ropes or two parts of the same rope, is a splice.

In choosing the right knot to use, the seaman should be guided simply by the purpose to be served. For in practice, with the exception of the splice, the various technical terms have become so blurred in meaning as to be virtually useless. For example, the so-called fisherman's bend is in fact a hitch, since it is used to hitch the rope to a ring or to a link in a chain.

The real key to the mystery of nautical knots is knowing when and where to tie each one—as explained in simplified language on the following pages. None of them is hard to master; in fact, with a modicum of practice all are remarkably easy—and useful. They share two other critical characteristics: properly made, none of them will slip or loosen on the job; and—again with the exception of the splice, which is intended to be permanent—they are all relatively easy to untie, even after being under heavy strain like the bowline at right.

A bowline tied in the clew of a genoa jib holds securely despite a 2,000-pound pull that has compressed the line to half its normal diameter. Even after such strains, the bowline is readily undone.

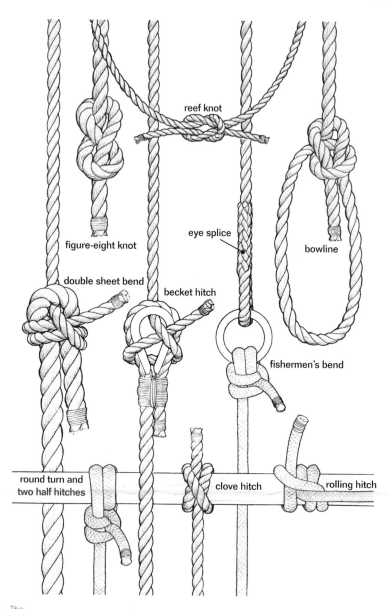

reef knot

figure-eight knot

eye splice

bowline

double sheet bend

becket hitch

fishermen's bend

round turn and
two half hitches

clove hitch

rolling hitch

Techniques for Tying

All of the knots shown on the following pages have certain fundamentals of structure in common. Together with a few definitions of rope parts, these fundamentals make up a simplified and useful vocabulary of knot tying as introduced below. Once the novice understands this vocabulary, it is only a small step to successful execution of the two most basic knots, the figure eight and the square, or reef, knot *(opposite)*.

Of these, by far the most familiar both to boatmen and landlubbers alike is the square knot. However, it is also the most unreliable. Though very useful for quickly tying together two rope ends of equal size, it is likely to slip and let go if attempted with ropes of unequal diameter. And unlike the other knots, the square knot sometimes jams on itself and becomes very hard to untie if wetted or put under heavy strain. In these latter conditions—common in storms when the knot is used for reefing—the variation shown in figure 5 on page 25 should be substituted.

The Vocabulary of Knots

Every knot is made up of rope parts interwoven into one or more loops. This weaving is carried out in specific over-and-under sequences. Below starts the rope parts and minor variations on the basic loop that form the structure of all knots.

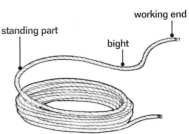

standing part

working end

bight

The end of the rope being used for knotting is the working end. A bight is any slack section in the middle part of the rope. The standing part is the main part of the rope, or that section of the rope about which the end is turned to form a knot, hitch, etc.

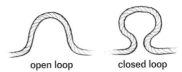

open loop   closed loop

A loop is a bight that forms at least a half circle. Bringing the end parts near each other forms a closed loop; leaving them apart makes an open one.

overhand turn   **underhand turn**

When the ends of a loop are crossed, the rope is said to have taken a turn. If the end is passed over the standing part, it is an overhand turn, and if passed under the standing part, it is an underhand turn.

overhand knot

When either end of a turn is put back through the loop, in an over-and-under sequence, the turn becomes a so-called overhand knot—which seamen do not regard as a proper knot but use, nonetheless, as a building block in making other knots.

eye

An eye is a loop made in a rope end and secured either by knotting or by the more permanent means of seizing—or splicing, as here.

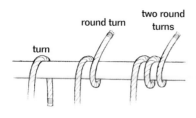

turn   **round turn**   **two round turns**

When a rope used in conjunction with another object, such as a spar or bollard, goes part way around the object, the rope is said to have taken a turn. If it goes completely around the object to form a closed loop, the rope makes a round turn. Two round turns are formed by passing the rope three times over the object to form two closed loops.

The Figure Eight

The figure-eight knot forms a solid lump in a line—either at the end or in a bight—that very effectively stops the line from running out too far through a block or fairlead. The figure eight also makes a quick temporary substitute for whipping the severed end of a line. To tie the figure eight, form an overhand loop and then take the end around and behind the standing part (1). Now pass the end up through the loop from front to back (2). To draw up, or tighten, the knot, pull on both ends (3). In making a stopper, never use the overhand knot, which can jam up so tightly that it must be cut off.

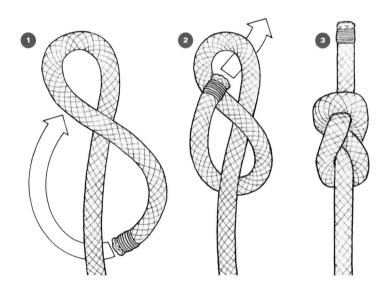

The Square Knot

The square knot, or reef knot, is the commonest device for binding together two ends of rope to enclose an object, such as the foot of a reefed sail. To tie it, hold one end still and work with the other. Pass the working end over (1) and then around and under the other, thus forming a simple overhand knot (2). Now turn both ends back and repeat the process; working with the same end as before, place it over (3), around and under. Draw up by pulling the ends (4). If quick release is vital, make a slipped reef (5) by using a bight or half bow, rather than an end, for the final step.

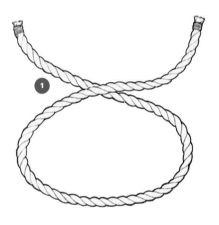

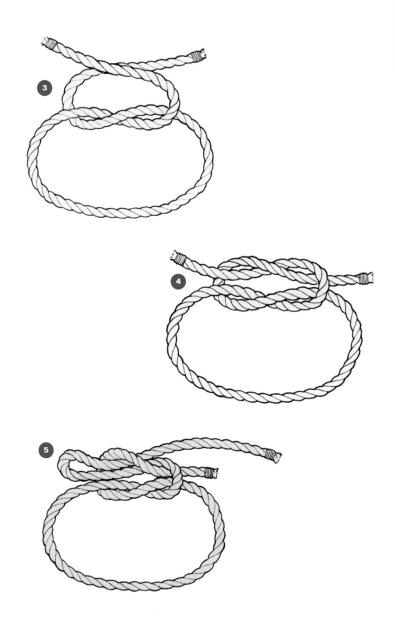

Tie a Bowline

The bowline is the seaman's most reliable and useful knot. A quick, strong method for making an eye in a line, the bowline never slips or jams. It can be tied in the end of a line or in the middle, with one loop or two, depending on the situation. In fact, if a sailor were able to learn only four knots in his life, this should be one of them (the others are the square, the half hitch, and the figure eight).

To tie a bowline, form an overhand loop; hold the junction firmly between the thumb and fingers of the right hand and turn over the right hand (1), palm up, to form a smaller loop with the working end sticking up through it (2). Hold the loop in the left hand and with the right lead the working end around behind the standing part (3), then forward and down through the small loop. The working end should finish inside the big loop, parallel to the right side. Pull down the working end and the right side of the big loop with one hand and the standing part with the other (4) to draw up the knot (5).

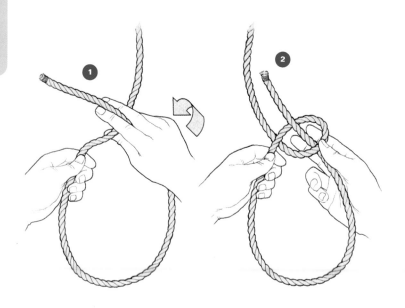

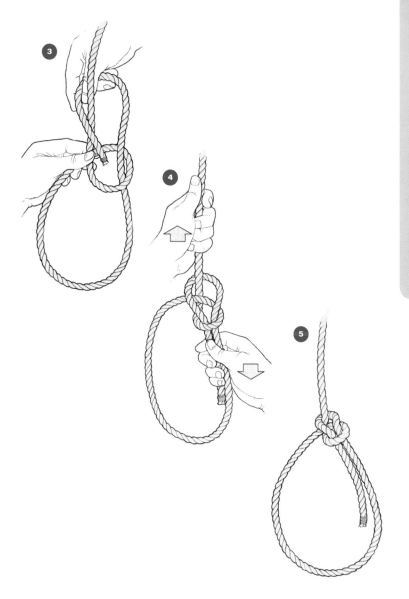

The Portuguese Bowline

One of the handiest of the specialized knots is a double-looped bowline called the Portuguese bend, which makes an excellent emergency bosun's chair for hoisting a person aloft to repair a mast. Its two interconnected loops can be adjusted after the knot is formed, so that one loop will fit around the person's chest and the other will make a sufficiently roomy seat. If it is properly tied, the knot will support the heaviest person aboard without either slipping or jamming.

1. To tie a Portuguese bowline, coil a pair of counterclockwise turns into a piece of line. Hold the coils securely with the left hand, and with the right hand grasp the point at which the line's working end crosses over the standing part, as shown. Then turn the right hand palm upward *(arrow)*, so that the working end passes first down behind the coils and then up through them.

2. Continue turning the right hand until the working end has been brought completely up through the two coils, and lies parallel with the standing part. You will have now created a small loop in the standing part, with the working end running up through it, as here.

3. Leading the working end of the line behind the standing part, then forward, bring it down over the two coils and back again through the small loop.

4. Grasp the working end and the right side of the inner coil in the right hand, and the standing part with the left, and pull in the direction of the arrows to draw the knot tight.

5. With the Portuguese bowline completed, its two continuous loops can be adjusted to any combination of sizes; and when a strain—like the weight of a man—goes onto the knot, neither of the loops will slip.

The Jug Sling

The jug sling is a special-purpose knot that originated ashore as a makeshift horse bridle, but has found particular usefulness in provisioning or unloading a boat. Drawn up tight around the mouth of a large water bottle, it forms a pair of reliable rope handles for hauling bulky liquid containers from shore to ship or vice versa.

1. The first step in tying a jug sling is to make a simple noose. This is most quickly done by fashioning an overhand knot with a bight from the standing part pulled through the turn, as above. Do not pull the overhand knot tight, and be sure the noose formed is a foot or more in diameter.

2. Make a secondary round turn within the noose by twisting its end so that one part of the line lies above the other, as shown above. Make this turn large enough so that you are able to bring it down and entirely encircle the loosely tied overhand knot *(arrow)*.

3. Now bring the bight of the original noose carefully over the enlarged round turn; then turn it downward toward you and weave it under the overhand knot *(arrow)*.

4. Draw the knot tight by grasping the loop of the noose in one hand, and the standing part and working end in the other; pull slowly and carefully in the direction of the arrows.

5. Cut the standing part of the line at a point equal to the remaining length of the working end. Then tie the two ends together with a square knot to form a loop equal in size to the loop from the noose. The two loops become the handle of the jug sling, while the strands in the center cinch tight in order to grasp the mouth of the bottle.

The Monkey's Fist

Besides being a highly ornamental knot, the monkey's fist serves the very practical purpose of weighting the end of a heaving line. The knot consists of three sets of interlocking round turns, with four turns in each set. When the knot has been completed—but not yet pulled tight—a small weight such as a lead ball, a stone or a golf ball is inserted into the middle. After being pulled tight, the fist can be finished off simply by splicing the leftover working end into the standing part. In this way, the fist becomes a permanent part of the heaving line.

Less conventional—but far more useful—is the finishing technique shown here, in which one turn from the monkey's fist is extended and then seized into a permanent loop. The monkey's fist can then be bent onto any heaving line as needed.

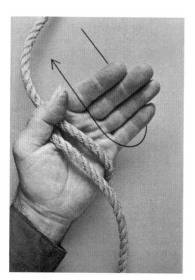

1. Begin work on the monkey's fist by laying the line across the palm of the left hand so that about 10 inches remain as the standing part. Secure the standing part with the base of your thumb; make a total of four turns with the working part around the hand in the direction of the arrow. This completes the first set of turns for the monkey's fist.

2. To start the second set, ease the first set down toward the fingertips, still gripping the turns with the thumb. The working end is now ready to be turned (*arrow*) around the first set and at right angles to it.

3. Grip the first of these turns for the second set with the thumb and forefinger. Wrap *(arrow)* the working end around the first set until there are four turns in the second set.

4. Now start the third set by tucking the working end through the first set of turns, as shown. Take care that the same tension has been kept on the line through each turn of each set so far, so that the knot retains a symmetrical shape.

5. To complete the third and final set of turns, rotate the left hand so the turns of the second set are vertical. Bring the working end up through the horizontal turns of the first set, next to the fingers. (This will add a fifth turn to the second set.) Cross the working end over the vertical turns outside them; again thread it through the horizontal turns *(arrow)*. Repeat until you have four turns.

6. Tuck the standing end *(arrow)* into the knot, thus creating a fourth turn on the side of the first set that had only three; now the monkey's fist is symmetrical, and the essential structure of the knot complete.

7. With your fingers, pry open a section of the knot at a junction of two rings; slip in the weight you have chosen—here a golf ball wrapped in twine for extra heft and bulk.

8. Start at either end of the line and tighten the knot around its heavy core. Use a marlinespike, as shown, advancing the slack (seen here looping upward) as you go. Work through the knot's entire structure again until you reach the third or middle turn of the five-part ring. Here, reserve enough slack—about 18 inches—to form a loop; keep tightening the knot on the other side of the loop.

9. Inspect the knot for tautness and firmness on all sides and, if necessary, work the turns again, adjusting the length of the loop handle until it approximates that shown above.

10. Cut off all excess line flush with the outside of the knot. The ends need not be whipped to prevent fraying; with use they will work back inside the knot altogether.

11. Finish the monkey's fist by wrapping a seizing for about an inch around the throat of the loop handle. This will prevent any part of the loop from working its way back into the knot and thus loosening it.

The Turk's Head

The elegant Turk's head makes a fine handgrip on the end of a tiller or on the top spoke of a ship's wheel. It can also be used as a ring for snubbing up the drawstrings of a duffel or ditty bag. A small one may even be laid flat to form a coaster on shipboard; a larger one can become a place mat.

Depending upon the purpose it is to serve and upon the diligence of the rope-worker, a Turk's head is structured of two or more parallel lines, or leads, worked into three or more bights or interweaving sections. A particularly popular form of the knot, with three leads and five bights, is shown here. Whatever the size, all Turk's heads are worked in the same way—a continuous under-over pattern executed one complete circle at a time.

1. To tie a Turk's head, lay the standing part of the line across the inside of the left hand so that the standing part—or bitter end—is down and the working part leads up and away from you. Wrap the working part around the hand and back across the first turn with the working part hanging behind, as shown.

2. Carry the working part up and over the first turn and weave it under the bight at right. Pull the entire length of the working end through the bight—as you will do in all subsequent weaving steps.

3. Now rotate the hand so that the palm faces out and the two turns of line run parallel across the backs of the fingers. Raise up the turn on the left and cross it over (*arrow*) the one on the right, as shown.

4. Bring the working end up and, approaching from the wrist side of the hand and going toward the fingers, weave it under the bight that is now on the left over the one on the right (*arrow*).

5. Weave the working end in the opposite direction (*arrow*), going under the turn on the right atop the little finger. Be sure to keep the knot very loose at this stage as you will need room to maneuver in later steps.

6. Inspect the knot at this point to see that each section of the knot is locked together by the interweaving of lines under or over each succeeding bight or turn, as shown. The basic construction of the Turk's head is now set.

7. Rotate the hand back to its palm-inward position. Start the second round in forming the knot by bringing the working end up under the line on the left side of the palm. Here, and in all subsequent steps, the working end as it comes through should lie to the right of the lead that it runs beside.

8. Turn the hand to the palm-outward position and continue to follow the lead established in the previous step, going under and over accordingly and always staying parallel and to the right of the lead.

9. When all parts of the knot have been doubled, as shown, begin the third circuit of the Turk's head. The pattern of placement remains the same, parallel and to the right of the leading line.

10. The weaving of the knot is completed when each of the five bights or turns consists of three parallel sections of line. Now tighten the knot, either on itself or on the spoke or post for which it is intended. Start at the working end and follow that single line toward the other end, pulling it snug, until you have circuited the knot three times.

11. To dispose of the two projecting ends, pull firmly on one of them and whip the extended end close to the knot. Now, cut off the line just beyond the whipping. Repeat the process with the other end and tuck both behind the interwoven bights. The finished knot now appears to have no beginning or end.

The Wall Knot

The wall knot is the basic building block for a series of more elaborate stopper knots and splices. It is the simplest of multistrand knots—those formed by unlaying a line and tying its strands. To make it, each strand in turn is passed *up* through a bight formed by the adjacent strand, as shown in the diagram at right.

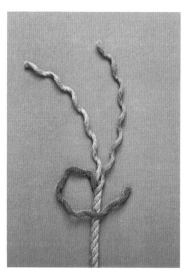

1. To start a wall, unlay about eight inches of line and hold the line in one hand with the strands pointing upward. With the other hand, turn the strand at the left *(red, above)* down toward you in a counterclockwise direction to form a bight, placing the end of the strand in front of the line's standing part.

2. Now turn the middle strand *(colorless)* counterclockwise through the bight of the first strand, forming a second bight identical with the first.

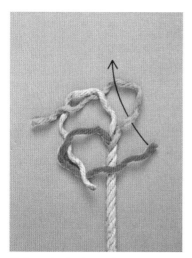

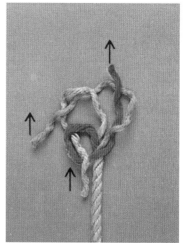

3. Pass the third strand *(yellow)* counterclockwise through the bight of the second strand *(colorless)*, forming a third bight. Finally, tuck the first strand up through this bight, as shown by the arrow.

4. Tug the strands—one by one, and little by little—in an upward direction *(arrows)*, slowly drawing the knot together and working it into its finished shape.

5. When pulled tight, the completed knot encircles the end of the standing part in three symmetrical bights. All three strands now point upward, ready to begin a new knot.

The Crown Knot

The crown knot, the reverse of the wall knot *(page 40)*, is often put on top of a wall; together they form an excellent stopper knot. The crown is formed by pulling each strand *down* through the bight of the next strand, and ends with the strands pointing downward. The crown is also used by itself to start a backsplice, or with a series of crowns to make a decorative braidwork called a crown sennit.

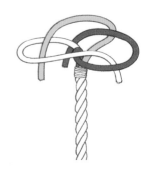

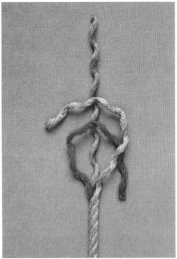

1. To make a crown alone, unlay the line and bring the left-hand strand *(red)* clockwise across the center strand *(yellow)* and down under the right-hand strand *(colorless)*.

2. Now pass the right-hand strand *(colorless)* counterclockwise over the center strand *(yellow)*, making a second bight similar to the first one.

3. Holding the second bight in place, begin the third bight *(yellow)* by looping the center strand counterclockwise and passing it down through the bight formed by the first *(red)* strand, as shown by the arrow.

4. With the final strand now caught under the bight that was formed by the first strand in the initial step, the knot is ready to be drawn into its final shape.

5. Work all three strands downward, slowly and carefully, tugging on them one at a time—firmly but not too hard—until the crown is closed tight.

The Tack Knot

The tack knot is a multistrand knob fashioned at the end of a line, where it makes a decorative and permanent terminal for a bell pull, a bucket lanyard or a handhold at the end of a strap hung next to the companionway ladder. The knot is built up by first tying a wall, then superimposing a crown, and finally leading each strand back through the knot to double both the wall and the crown. An old sailors' ditty describes the process: "First a wall, then a crown; Now tuck up, then tuck down."

Each of the steps shown at right should be done with the knot kept fairly loose, so that the strands can be woven through easily when doubling. Even so, a marlinespike will be necessary for the last series of tucks, in which the strands are led down through the knot's center, parallel with the standing part.

1. Lay open the rope for about 12 inches, and whip the throat and the ends of the strands. Make a wall knot, and then fashion a crown *(preceding pages)* directly on top of the wall. Leave each knot fairly loose. Then take one strand *(red)* and tuck it back up through the knot *(arrow)*, following the lead of the nearest strand in the wall knot; the new tuck will lie below the old lead and parallel to it.

2. Continue doubling the wall knot, tucking each strand in turn, in each case following below and parallel to the original lead. Thus, in this example, the red strand will follow the red lead, and the yellow strand the yellow lead. End with the strands pointing upward; prepare to make the first tuck for doubling the crown *(arrow)*.

3. To double the crown, you must open a passageway through the center of the knot for each strand. Insert the tip of the marlinespike between an edge of the crown and the adjacent lead of the doubled wall; push it down next to the standing part. Remove the marlinespike; tuck the doubling strand beside the first crown's lead and down through the opening. Repeat for each strand.

4. When all the strands have been tucked down through the knot, start working them tight. Begin by systematically drawing up each strand in the original wall, then tightening each strand in the original crown, then drawing up the doubling strands in sequence.

5. Finally, cut off each strand where it emerges from the knot. Alternately finish the knot by tapering the strands, backsplicing them into the standing part and then covering the splice with a serving.

The Matthew Walker

Another handsome terminal knot with much the same uses as the tack knot is the Matthew Walker. One of the oldest of multistrand knots—mention of it appears in British admiralty records as early as 1644—it was utilized in old sailing ships as a stopper knot to keep a line from reeving out through a deadeye. Today it adds a distinctive element to any number of ropeworking projects, such as making a lanyard or a ditty bag.

1. Lay open about 12 inches of rope; whip the throat and the end of each strand to avoid fraying. Arrange the strands in crescents going counterclockwise. Bring the left-hand strand *(red)* around the standing part and pull it through its own bight, forming an overhand knot. Then prepare to make a similar overhand knot around the standing part with the center strand.

2. Bring the center strand forward over the tip of the first strand, below the first bight and around the standing part. It will form its own bight; lead the end back up through this bight and the previous one for the second overhand knot. Repeat with the third strand *(yellow)*, leading the end through its own bight and the two previous ones for a third overhand knot around the standing part.

3. The end of each strand should now emerge from the knot through its own bight. Begin working the knot into shape by gently pulling each strand upward in turn.

4. As you work the knot, arrange each turn symmetrically around the standing part. Be careful to tighten each strand a little bit at a time, moving methodically on to the next strand, so as not to pull the knot askew.

5. Lay up the three strands for a distance of ½ inch or more, as desired, from the knot and whip them together. Cut off the ends about ¼ inch up from the whipping.

CHAPTER 4:
Tying to Lines and Rings

Every sailor should know how to secure lines firmly to other lines—and to permanent eyes and ring fittings. The bends and hitches shown here are particularly suited to these purposes. Each is quickly tied, notably strong, and reliable even under the heaviest strain. And with the exception of the fisherman's bend, each is easy to untie, even when a wet line that has been under strain is being worked with. However, because the fisherman's bend is primarily used for tying a rope to an anchor ring, security of the knot takes priority over ease of undoing.

Knowing how to tie a knot quickly can be the difference between the safety and security of crew and belongings and losing something overboard.

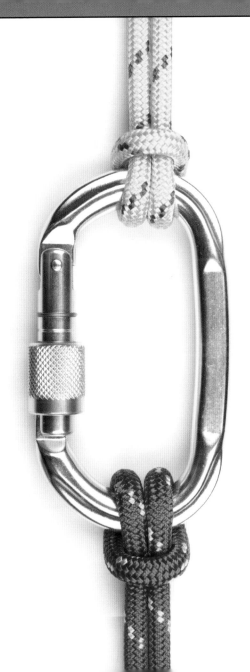

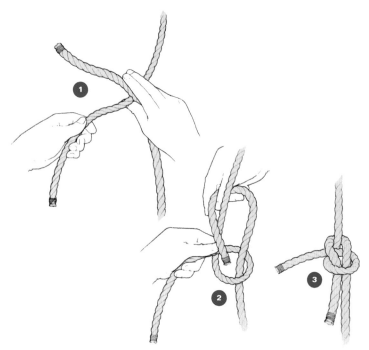

The quickest, most reliable way to tie two rope ends together—even with lines of unequal size—is by making a sheet bend using the method shown here. Cross the working end of the heavier rope over the lighter. Grasp the crossed lines as shown (1) and twist them—as in making a bowline—to form a small loop, with the end coming up through it. Pass the end around behind the standing part and back down through the loop (2). Draw up carefully and tightly (3) before putting any strain on the line.

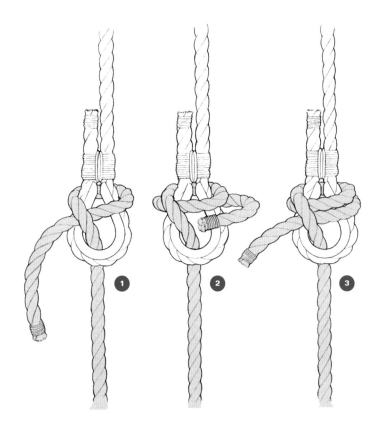

The becket hitch ties a line to a becket, i.e., any permanently closed loop. Start by passing the line end up through the becket, then take it around behind the loop and pass it back under itself (1). If the eye is large, double the hitch by taking another turn around the becket and again passing the working end under itself (2 and 3).

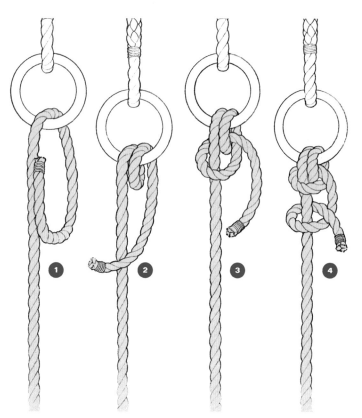

The fisherman's bend, also known as the anchor bend, is the most widely used means of tying a line onto a metal ring—often, as the alternate name implies, to an anchor ring. To tie the bend, take a round turn (1 and 2) around the ring. Pass the end through both parts of the turn (3)—in effect, putting in a half hitch—and pull tight. Secure the end with another half hitch (4).

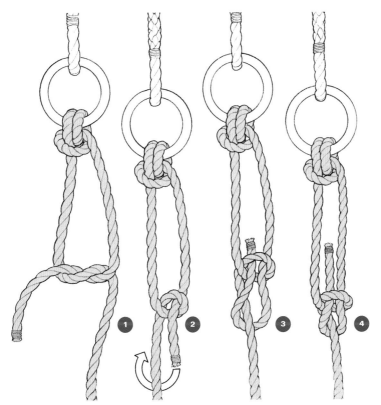

A bowline combined with a fisherman's bend gives extra security and lessens jamming during long underwater use. Instead of ending the knot with the second half hitch, take the end of the line and turn it around the standing part from front to back, forming a loop with an overhand knot at the bottom (1). Give the free end a sharp downward pull, causing the overhand knot to roll over and form a small loop in the standing part (2). Pass the free end behind the standing part and up through the loop (3), as in a regular bowline. Draw up carefully so pressure is equal on both parts and the knot is secure (4).

The Adaptable Hitch

The most convenient and versatile way to tie a rope to any object, whether a spar, rail, bollard, or shroud, is the hitch. Hitches are of two main types: those that effectively resist a pull parallel to the object and those that resist a perpendicular strain. Both come into daily use aboard ship for suspending weights, docking, or cleating. The basic conformation in all hitches is the single hitch, which is not a true knot in itself but a building block or security turn in other knots.

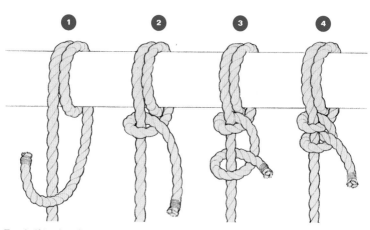

Two half hitches form the best quick-tying knot for suspending a weight perpendicularly from a rail. To tie it, take a round turn (1), bring the end in front of the standing part and through the loop in a half hitch (2). Then make a second half hitch (3); draw tight (4).

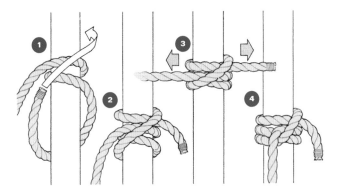

A rolling hitch is often used to secure the safety line of a bosun's chair to a mast, for the knot holds firm when the strain on the standing part is parallel to the object to which it is tied. Moreover, it is most effective on a smooth surface. To tie the basic rolling hitch, take two turns around the object (1). Bring the end up and over the turns; make another turn at the top and pass the end back under itself in a single hitch (2). Push the turns together and draw the knot tight (3). Strain on the standing part (4) will now force the diagonal to roll over and the knot's grip will be tightened.

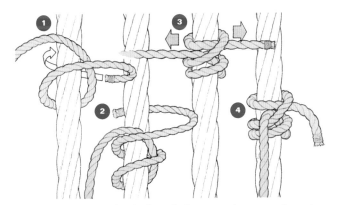

An alternate version of the rolling hitch—called a stopper by some sailors—is used for tying a weight to another line such as a wire shroud, which offers less surface for the knot to grip. Begin by taking a round turn (1), but ensure that the second part of the turn runs above the first to nip it against the shroud. Next take the end around the shroud again, and over the standing part again (2). Finish by tucking the end under in a single hitch. Set up carefully, pushing the turns together and drawing up tight (3), before placing strain on the line (4).

The easy-tying clove hitch, which holds well under a steady strain perpendicular to the object on which it is tied, is perfect as a quick mooring knot, whether to a rail *(above)* or to a bollard *(below and opposite)*. To tie the clove hitch to a rail, take one turn (1) and then make a second that crosses the standing part (2). Pass the end up under the second turn in a single hitch (3). Note, however, that the knot begins to come undone under a sideways strain (4).

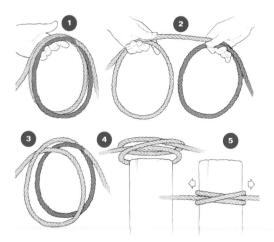

When a boat's crew wants to make a quick fastening to a bollard or piling, the best knot is a clove hitch tied in hand, that is, completed loosely before being dropped over the object. To tie the clove hitch in the hand, take two loops in the left hand (1); pass the second loop around behind the first (2 and 3), thus forming both an overhand and an underhand loop. Slip both loops over the bollard (4) and tighten the knot with even pressure on both ends (5). This method is particularly convenient when a boat whose lines have no eyes is temporarily docked.

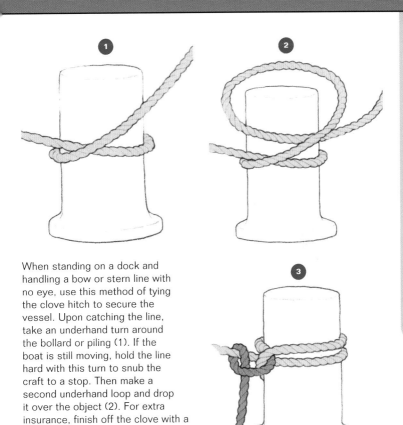

When standing on a dock and handling a bow or stern line with no eye, use this method of tying the clove hitch to secure the vessel. Upon catching the line, take an underhand turn around the bollard or piling (1). If the boat is still moving, hold the line hard with this turn to snub the craft to a stop. Then make a second underhand loop and drop it over the object (2). For extra insurance, finish off the clove with a half hitch around the line's standing part (3).

CHAPTER 5:
Splicing

The best way to form a permanent loop in a dock line or any other piece of rope is by making an eye splice. And though rope manufacturers provide line with ready-made splices, many sailors avoid the size limitations and costs of the standardized product by making their own.

It takes no more than 20 minutes to splice a fiber or nylon line of standard three-strand, half-inch rope, such as that shown at right. The loop can be tailored to the size of the cleats and bollards most likely to be encountered.

When finished, a splice barely weakens the line at all: 5 to 10 percent compared to the 30 to 40 percent of a bowline. Finally, the splice is particularly satisfying to make. Even the most seasoned sailors take pride in their splices, often tapering them by progressively trimming fibers off the strands as they weave.

The boatman can ensure a neat splice by whipping the rope strands with constrictor knots. To tie a constrictor, use whipping cord and take two turns around the strand, holding the second turn open with the left index finger (1). Take the working end between the right thumb and index finger, transfer the loop to the right middle finger (2) and pass the working end through both turns (3). Tighten from both ends (4, 5), easing the second turn down to bind the first.

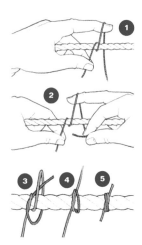

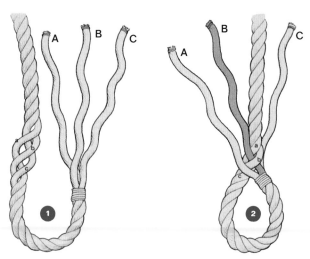

(1) Whip the rope about eight inches from the end and unlay the strands A, B, and C. Whip each strand end *(below, left)*. Form an eye and open up the strands a, b, and c in the standing part. (2) Lay the working end over the standing part with A on top and to the left. Tuck B under b, from right to left, and pull it through.

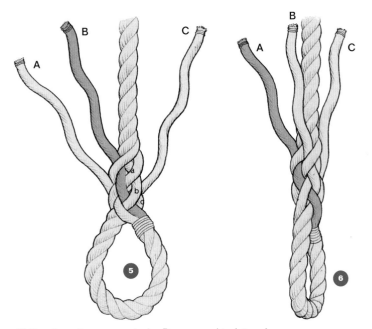

(5) Turn the splice over again; lay B over a and tuck it under the next strand. Continue the process (6) with A and—rotating the splice—with strand C (7), passing each strand in turn over one strand in the standing part and tucking it under the next. As you rotate, pull and twist each strand in sequence to maintain even tension and lay.

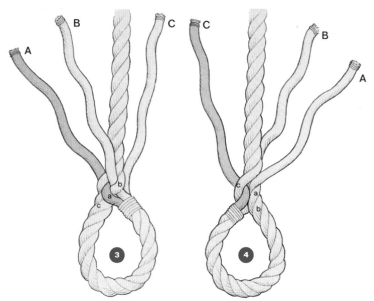

(3) Bring A over b, tuck it under a, and pull it through until its tension matches that on B. As you work, maintain the lay of the strands by twisting each clockwise as you pull it through. (4) Turn the splice over and tuck the final strand, C, under c, from right to left. Tucks are always taken from right to left, against the lay of the rope.

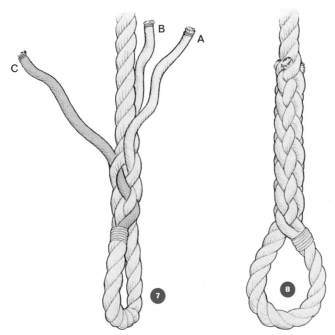

C

B

A

7

8

To finish, in natural fiber continue for at least three more tucks; use five more tucks in synthetics. Then cut off the ends. With fiber, leave half-inch tag ends, which will work themselves back in and hold. With synthetics, fuse the ends to prevent them from slipping out. Roll the finished splice (8) in the hands or underfoot to even it out.

The Back Splice

The back splice was originally conceived as a strong, durable means of ending off a line when, on typically long windjammer voyages, whipping cord was not available to sailors. For today's recreational boatman, it makes a firm handle for a bell rope, a lead line, or a bucket rope.

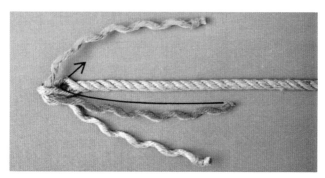

1. To make a back splice, unlay the line about six inches and make a crown knot *(pages 42–43)*. Pick up any of the three loose strands *(here, the red one)* and, moving against the lay of the rope, loop the loose strand over the nearest strand of the standing part of the rope, under the next one *(arrow)*, and pull it through. Give the rope a one-third turn away from yourself, pick up the next strand *(uncolored)* and loop it over the first standing strand and under the next. Turn the rope again, and repeat with the yellow strand.

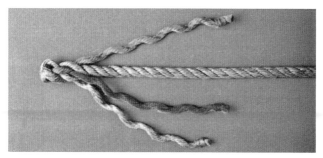

2. After all three strands have been tucked once through the standing part of the rope, take another complete set of tucks in the standing part, putting the loose strands through it one by one, as before. Use a fid or a marlinespike as needed to pry openings in the standing part.

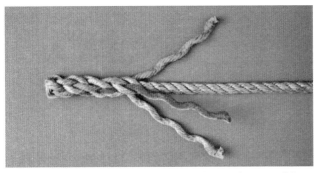

3. When three full tucks have been taken through the standing part of the rope, pull all strands taut—making certain that all are in equal tension—and twist each one with the lay of the strand. Cut the loose strands off, leaving an end of about ¾ inch on each.

4. After the strand ends have been cut off, roll the splice between the palms of your hands or underfoot; this procedure will push the strands and their fibers together so as to make the splice a smooth one. The rope now has a finished end that can be easily gripped.

The Short Splice

The short splice is a stout way of permanently joining two lines of equal material and diameter, and thus lengthening dock lines, towing lines, anchor rodes and the like. However, the splice forms a bulge that is double the rope's normal diameter, so should never be used for lines that are intended to run through a block or eye.

1. To make a short splice, unlay the strands of two line ends for six to eight inches. Interlace the three strands from one line with the three strands of the other, as shown, so each strand lies between two of the opposite line. This is called "marrying" the two lines. Put a temporary seizing around the marry where the six strands come together.

2. After you have married the two lines, take any loose strand (*in the picture above, the red one*) from the left-hand line, pass it over the nearest strand of the right-hand line, then tuck it under the next strand—going against the lay as in the back splice (*pages 64–65*). Give both of the lines a one-third turn away from you and proceed in the same manner with the next loose strand (*yellow*) and finally with the third (*uncolored*) strand. Take three complete tucks in all.

3. Cut off the seizing and flip the rope so that the part in which the three tucks have been taken now lies to the left. Pull the remaining three loose strands tight and work them, one at a time, through the rope as before—each strand going against the lay, first over and then under a standing strand. Make three complete tucks.

4. Cut the ends off all six strands, leaving about ¾ inch protruding. Roll the splice between the palms of your hands or underfoot until the protruding strand ends have been pressed into the splice and are no longer visible. The two lines have now been joined into one, and are ready for use.

The Long Splice

The long splice joins two lengths of line so smoothly that the splice will run through a block or any other type of fair-lead. Essentially the simplest of all splices to execute, it is weaker than a short splice, but has the advantage of not significantly increasing the diameter of the lines at the point where the two are laid together.

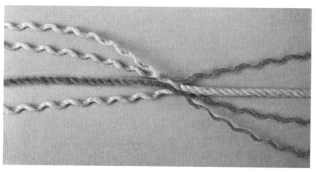

1. To make a long splice, unlay two ropes at least 15 inches for each half inch of the lines' circumference. Then marry the strands *(above)*, joining the two unlaid lines together, end to end, so that the strands of one pass between the strands of the other.

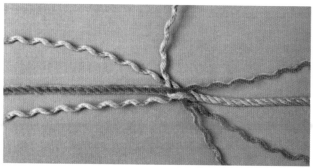

2. At the marry, take any two corresponding strands—say, the center strand of each line *(here, the left-hand line and its strands are tinted brown for easy identification)*—and tie an overhand knot. Leave the knot just loose enough to be readjusted later during splicing.

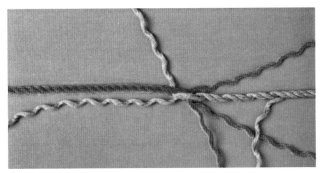

3. Take one of the unknotted strands *(shown untinted)* and unlay it away from the marry; here the chosen strand has been unlaid back down the right-hand line. For clarity and simplicity, the strand at right has been unlaid only a few turns; in making a serviceable splice, however, the strand should be unlaid some 10 or 12 inches for each half inch of the rope's circumference.

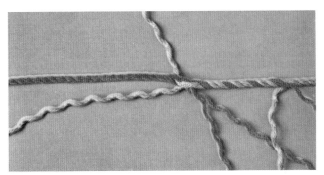

4. Now take from the left-hand line the strand corresponding to the one just unlaid, and lay it into the spiraled groove left open by the unlaying. Stop when you reach the end of the groove, and the two strands meet; both should have bitter ends of three or four inches.

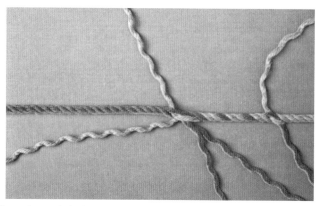

5. Where the newly laid strand meets its counterpart, make an overhand knot and pull it tight. Then go back to the crotch, smoothing the new-laid strand in its groove as you go, and pull the crotch knot tight. Make sure that both knots have equal tension, and that the tension is sufficient to snug the strands down into the line but not enough to cause bunching or an uneven lay anywhere on the line.

6. From the left-hand line, unlay the remaining unknotted strand another 10 or 12 inches for each half inch of the rope's circumference and, in the groove it leaves, lay in its counterpart from the right. Where the two strands meet, tie another overhand knot and pull it tight.

7. Make sure that all laid and re-laid strands have equal tension. Then return to the crotch and the first knot you tied. Take two snug tucks with each of its loose strands, working each one over, then under, then over and under again, the strand nearest to it in the standing part of the rope. Snip off the ends, leaving a quarter of an inch.

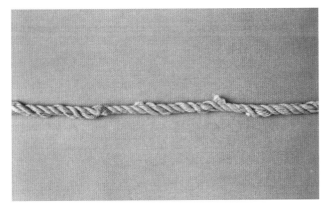

8. Take two tucks with each dangling strand at both ends of the splice and snip each end off a quarter of an inch from the rope. Then roll the rope between your palms or underfoot, smoothing each of the knots you have made. The finished splice should have three inconspicuous bumps where you have made the overhand knots.

The Braided Eye Splice

To make an eye splice in braided line, special tools and techniques are required.

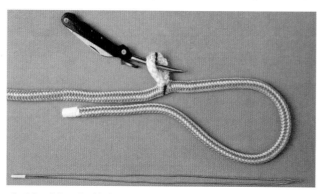

1. Bend a 36-inch length of baling wire into a fid, as shown; tape the ends. Tape the working end of the braided line and tie an overhand knot four feet from the tip. Form a loop the size of the desired eye; pencil a hatch mark on the cover at the point where the splice should begin. Bend the line here, pry apart the cover with a marlinespike and extract a short loop of the core. Mark the core where it emerges from the cover.

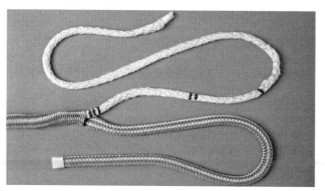

2. Pull the rest of the core from the working end of the cover. Then continue extracting the core from the standing part—pushing back the cover as you go—until you have pulled out an additional 10 inches. Tape the tip of the core. Starting at the hatch mark made on the core, measure off four inches and designate the spot with two pencil marks, as shown. From this double hatch mark, measure six inches to the junction with the cover; identify this spot with three hatch marks.

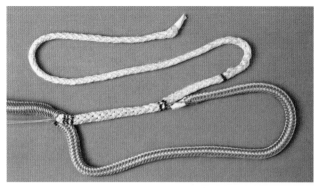

3. Now comes the actual splicing procedure of running the cover into the core with the fid. Insert the looped end of the fid into the hollow core at the triple hatch mark, thread it through the core and push it out at the double mark. Tightly retape the tip of the cover to give it a point. Slip this tip into the head of the fid so that two to three inches of line are gripped securely between the wires, as shown.

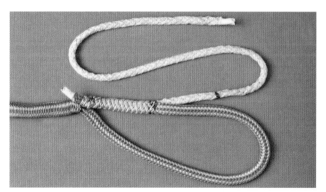

4. Pull the fid back through the core, drawing the cover with it. This may take considerable effort, since the core's diameter is smaller than the diameter of the cover. But by wiggling the fid back and forth you should be able to force the cover through. Keep pulling until the cover's taped tip emerges at the triple pencil mark. Detach the cover from the fid and work the taped tip back into the core.

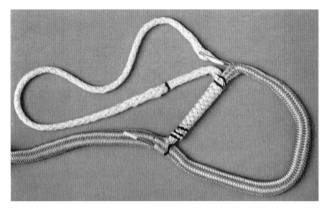

5. Next, the exposed portion of core will be threaded back into the cover. Begin by inserting the fid into the cover about one half inch below the cover's hatch mark. Make the insertion carefully so the fid does not pick up fibers from the adjacent core. Run the fid through the loop made by the empty cover and bring it out as close as you can to the point where you have just threaded the cover into the core. Now wedge the tip of the core into the head of the fid. Pull on the fid to draw the core back into the cover, as shown.

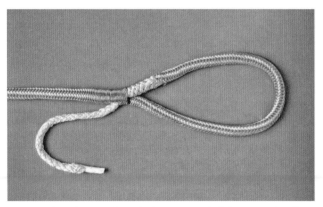

6. Continue to draw the core through the cover until all the excess has been fed through. Detach the fid and smooth out the loop to ease any bulges. Then start working the bunched portion of the cover—which you pushed back into the standing part in the second step *(page 72)*—forward over the throat of the eye.

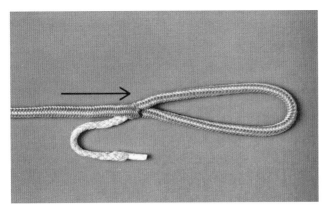

7. To bring the cover over the bulkiest part of the throat, grab the rope with one hand at the overhand knot you tied in the first step. With the other hand, grip the cover just above the knot and push it up toward the splice *(arrow)*. A sharp, jerking motion is sometimes required to force the cover over the thickest sections of the throat.

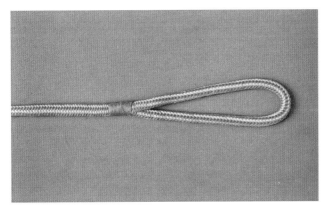

8. Snip off the tail of the core about one eighth of an inch from the cover. Hold the loop in one hand and the standing part in the other and pull; this pressure on the splice simulates the strain it will be under when in use, and helps to even out the cover. To make sure that the splice will be tight and will not work loose when the line is slack, seize the throat with waxed nylon. The seizing should cover about three inches from the bottom of the loop down the throat.

CHAPTER 6:
Additional Uses

Being comfortable on a boat is as much about having the right tools as it is about having the right skills. In a couple hours, a skilled boatman can create a sturdy rope ladder *(page 82)* useful in pulling in a lost sailor or swimmer or climbing skyward to perform necessary repairs. He can thread together a knife lanyard to ensure that he always has a rigging knife available *(page 86)*. And that same boatman will use similar knot skills to tie off to a cleat or bitt *(page 90)*.

A Coachwhipped Wheel

For all its trim appearance and sturdy functionality, the shiny metal-rimmed wheel that has become standard equipment on most modern boats of any size has certain practical drawbacks. It can become almost unmanageably slippery when wetted by a rain squall or by windblown spray, and in cold weather it is likely to be icy to the touch. However, by wrapping the rim with cotton seine twine—or any similar small-diameter, hard-laid line—the boatman can produce a nonslip surface of relatively constant temperature. Moreover, a neatly wrapped wheel acquires a distinctly salty look, and the wrapping technique is simplicity itself, involving as it does only a single elementary knot—the familiar half hitch.

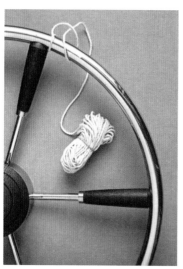

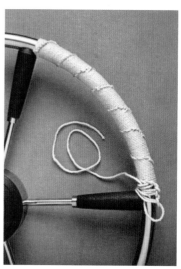

1. Take the bitter end from a skein of cotton line and lay about six inches along the wheel rim. Starting to the right of a spoke, wind the skein around the rim in a series of half hitches *(above)*, burying the bitter end as you go. Make the hitches in a clockwise direction, passing the working end through each successive turn from right to left.

2. As you finish a segment of rim, make the last few hitches loosely; pass the working end of the line back through these hitches *(above)*, then tighten the hitches and trim off the working end. If all the half hitches have been made alike, the points at which the line passes over itself will fall automatically into a symmetrical spiral pattern, as above.

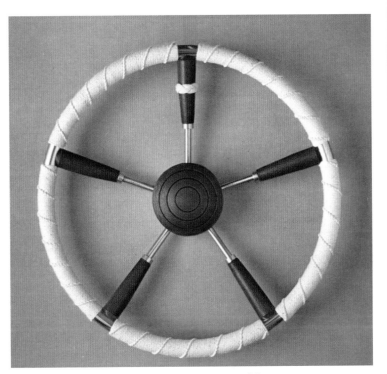

3. Continue in the same way to wrap each segment of the rim between one spoke and the next until all segments have been covered. As a final touch, determine which spoke is vertical and uppermost when the boat's rudder is amidships, and tie a Turk's head *(pages 36–39)* around that spoke to serve as a handy reference for the helmsman.

A Spliced Bridle

A water-ski bridle functions as a strong and flexible link between a skier's towline and the towboat. The bridle attaches to a pair of eyebolts, one fixed on either side of the transom. Threaded into the bridle is a lightweight running block, with a shackle for attaching the towline. As the skier slaloms from one side to the other, the running block slides along the bridle so that the drag on each section of line remains equal—so long as neither the skier nor the boat driver turns too abruptly.

While bridles like the one shown here are commercially available in various sizes, a boatman can fashion his own from braided polyethylene water-ski towline, suiting it exactly to his boat's dimensions—and the process will take him no more than 10 minutes' working time.

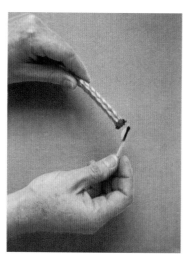 

1. A bridle requires enough ⁵⁄₁₆-inch hollow-core polyethylene line to reach from one eyebolt on the towboat's transom to the other, with enough slack to clear the boats outboard motor or drive unit by about six inches—plus additional line to form two eye splices. Begin the bridle by burning each of the line's two ends with a match *(above)* until the strands have fused together.

2. Thread a pair of sister hooks onto one end of the line. Open up a segment of line about 16 inches from the working end by grasping the line about an inch on either side of the selected spot and squashing the line together. At least one opening will appear between the woven braids. Insert the working end into the line's hollow interior *(above)*; push three or four inches of the end back inside the line.

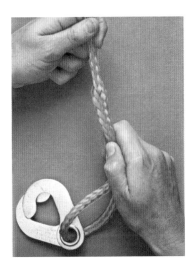

3. Now grasp the line just above the splice with one hand and below the splice with the other. Pull hard on the splice, as shown. Since polyethylene line stretches and attenuates slightly under tension, the grip of the strands surrounding the working end will tighten as tension increases. The harder the pull on the splice, the stronger it grows.

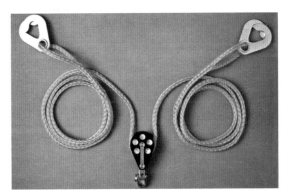

4. Thread onto the line a small lightweight block with a swiveling shackle. Then complete the project by attaching a pair of sister hooks at the other end of the line with an eye splice made the same way as the first. The finished bridle can be clipped securely to the boat by the sister hooks. The water-ski towline attaches to the shackle on the end of the block. To make sure that the weight of the block will not sink the bridle far enough to foul the propeller, fasten a small plastic float onto the towline near its juncture with the block.

A Rope Ladder

A boatman with an hour to spare can contrive a sturdy rope ladder topped off with a chafe-guarded eye for attaching a line. To calculate the amount of manila needed, simply double the desired length of the ladder and add three feet for each rung. The only other material required is a hank of hard-twisted jute for putting a serving of round turns over the eye to bind it securely.

The finished ladder has a variety of uses aboard a boat. It can be slung over the side in a matter of seconds; its round rungs offer firm and comfortable support to a swimmer's bare feet; and it coils neatly away in a deck locker when not in use. A sailor making repeated trips up the mast in the course of a repair job may also find such a ladder a handy alternative to the bosun's chair.

1. Start the ladder by making the eye. In the middle of the manila line, make a loop three to four inches long. Lay a strand of jute along the left side of the loop and parallel with it, so that the strand's bitter end points toward the top of the loop. Starting near the throat of the loop, bind the rope with jute, covering the bitter end of the jute as you go.

2. After binding the loop of the eye, continue wrapping jute around the two strands of rope, seizing them together for an inch or so to secure the throat of the eye. Leave a little slack in the last few turns so that you can pass the working end of the jute up under them. Draw these final turns tight around the working end, and cut off any excess jute.

3. To form the first rung of the ladder, first measure down 10 inches from the throat of the eye. Take the left-hand leg of the ladder and loop it around the right leg. Then pull another loop across to the left. To hold the loops in place, it will help if you lay out the work against a board and drive a nail next to the line, as shown, wherever you change the direction of the lead.

4. With the working end of the right leg, take enough round turns around the two bights to make a rung five or six inches wide. Work from right to left, and be sure that each turn is snugged up tightly against its neighbors.

5. When the last turn of the first rung has been completed, pull the working end of the right leg through the loop of the left-hand bight. Note that the right leg has now become the left, and vice versa. Remove the finished rung from the nails and draw the parts up tight. Continue making rungs every 10 inches, taking care to keep the intervals between rungs the same length on both sides.

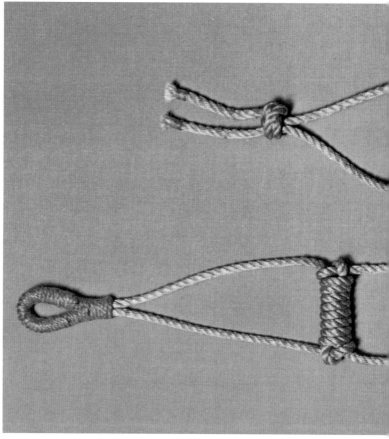

6. After finishing the last rung, secure the working ends of the two legs together. The ends can simply be spliced to each other, but a handsomer finale can be achieved, as shown here, by tying a two-strand Matthew Walker knot and then whipping the ends of the two ropes with marline.

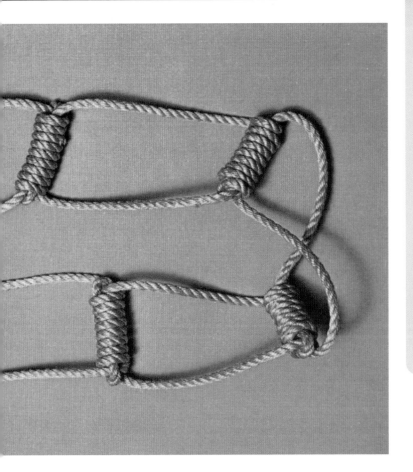

A Knife Lanyard

No sailor should ever be caught without his rigging knife, and a decorative assurance that the knife will always be by his side is a lanyard like the one shown on page 89. Knotted out of seine twine, it has a loop at one end for threading it into a belt, and a similar loop at the other end for the snap hook that holds the knife. Between the Turk's heads at the throats of the loops are a series of square knots. The work's intricate appearance belies its simplicity—anyone who can tie his shoes can make a lanyard in an afternoon.

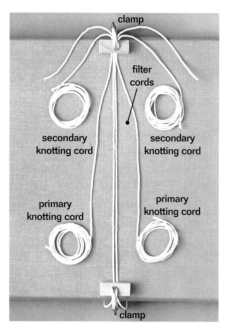

clamp

filter
cords

secondary
knotting cord

secondary
knotting cord

primary
knotting cord

primary
knotting cord

clamp

1. To begin making a knife lanyard, clamp side by side, as shown, the bottom ends of two 4-foot lengths of seine twine. These are the filler cords. Clamp the top ends of the filler cords similarly, enclosing in the same clamp and alongside the filler cords the mid-points of two 14-foot lengths of twine. The bottom ends of these two additional lengths of twine are called primary cords; the top ends are the secondary knotting cords. Secure the clamps so the filler cords are stretched taut, as shown at right. You are now ready to start knotting the lanyard.

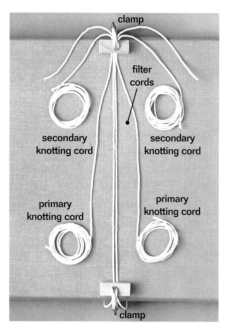 sidebar: 6: ADDITIONAL USES

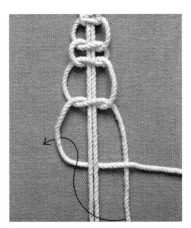 

2. To make the belt loop, tie a series of square knots around the filler cords with the primary knotting cords. Pass the working end of the left-hand knotting cord over the fillers and under the right-hand knotting cord; then pass the right cord under the fillers and through the bight of the left cord. To complete the knot reverse the lead of the knotting cords, as indicated by the arrow.

3. When the belt-loop section is as long as you want it, unclamp the work. Cut away the filler cords from each end of the knotted strip, sealing the cut ends with dabs of glue. Bring the ends of the strip together to form a loop. Using the two primary knotting cords as a new set of filler cords, tie 10 square knots with the secondary knotting cords.

4. Now tie 20 half-knots around the new filler cords. Each half-knot is tied, as shown above *(arrow)*, exactly like its predecessor, instead of reversing the lead as in the square knot. The 20 half-knots form a spiral section of lanyard, as shown at left. Follow the half-knots with 10 square knots, then 20 more half-knots, then a final section of 10 square knots.

5. Next, make the section that will form the knife loop. At this point, all four cords become knotting cords. Tie them into a series of four-strand crown knots. This knot is made like the three-strand crown knot *(pages 42–43)*, with each strand passing through a bight of the next strand *(above)*. The resulting chain of knots, designed to resist wear, is known as a four-strand crown sennit.

6. Thread onto the section of sennit a snap hook for attaching your knife. Form the sennit into a loop, and with two of the four cords used to make the section, tie three or four square knots around the lanyard at the throat of the loop. Trim all four ends and dab with glue.

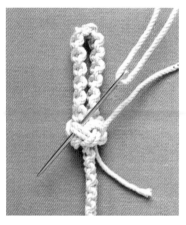

7. Tie Turk's head knots *(pages 36–39)* around the throats of the belt loop and the knife loop, using the same seine twine employed in making the lanyard. To ease the task of making these small Turk's heads, manipulate the twine with a blunt darning needle, as shown at left, instead of trying to guide the working end of the twine by hand.

8. The completed lanyard *(above)* is a strong and seamanly piece of ropework made interesting by its varied textures. It is long enough to permit free use of the knife but not so long as to be an encumbrance to the wearer.

Cleats for Belaying

A stout cleat provides a quick, sure way to make fast a line—and hold it, no matter how great the strain. The commonest cleat, used for holding down anything from a mainsheet to a mooring line, consists of two arms, or horns, attached to a base, which should be screwed or bolted to the boat. A line being secured to a standard cleat is wrapped, or belayed, in a series of figure eights *(right)*.

A good seaman can belay a line on a standard cleat in two or three seconds. But specialized, fast-acting cleats developed for racing make belaying virtually instantaneous. Jam cleats snag the line in a sharp V under one arm, or horn, and cam cleats grip the line between two swiveling serrated jaws *(below)*. Both cam and jam cleats release a line just as quickly—making them useful for mainsheets and jib sheets, which demand frequent adjusting.

Mooring lines and most halyards are usually made fast to standard cleats, and secured with a final half hitch to prevent the belay from accidentally unwinding. On some larger boats the bow cleat is replaced by a bitt *(page 93)*, which will hold a heavy hawser in rough seas.

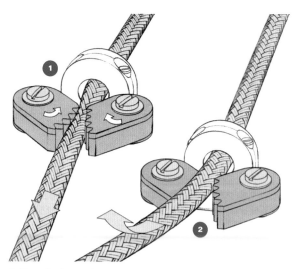

1. To make fast with a cam cleat, haul the line over the center of the cleat (1) and press it down against the tops of the spring-loaded cams, spreading them apart so the line drops between them. When the cams swivel back *(small arrows)* they bite the line and hold it. To let go the line (2), tug it back and upward.

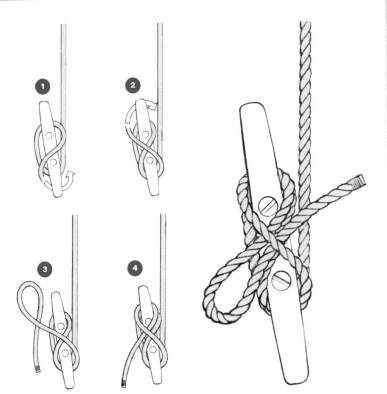

2. To belay a line to a standard cleat, wrap it once around the cleat's base (1), then lead it over the top of the cleat and around the lower horn (2) to form a figure eight. Make one more figure eight and finish with an underhand loop (3), which is passed over the upper horn to form a half hitch (4). The half hitch may be made with a half bow *(above, right)* for quick release. When cleating sheets, some boatmen omit the half hitch and finish with a turn around the cleat's base.

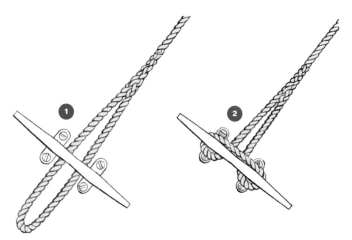

3. Most mooring cleats are open at the base to allow the spliced-in loops of mooring lines to be made fast easily. To do so, feed the eye through the opening (1), then loop it back over both horns and pull the line taut (2). Another eye can be looped to the same cleat if led through from the opposite direction.

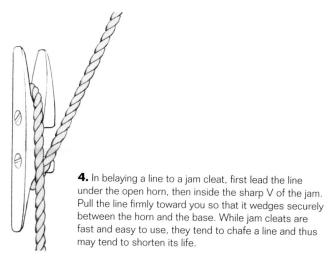

4. In belaying a line to a jam cleat, first lead the line under the open horn, then inside the sharp V of the jam. Pull the line firmly toward you so that it wedges securely between the horn and the base. While jam cleats are fast and easy to use, they tend to chafe a line and thus may tend to shorten its life.

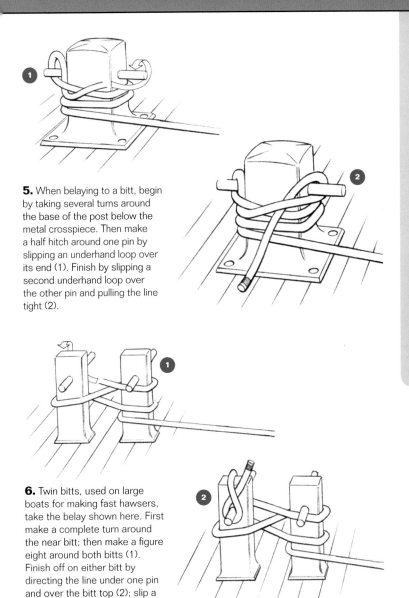

5. When belaying to a bitt, begin by taking several turns around the base of the post below the metal crosspiece. Then make a half hitch around one pin by slipping an underhand loop over its end (1). Finish by slipping a second underhand loop over the other pin and pulling the line tight (2).

6. Twin bitts, used on large boats for making fast hawsers, take the belay shown here. First make a complete turn around the near bitt; then make a figure eight around both bitts (1). Finish off on either bitt by directing the line under one pin and over the bitt top (2); slip a half hitch over the opposite pin.

Index

| c: chart |
| i: illustration |
| p: photos |

The Essential Guide to
Boating Series

Seamanship
A Beginner's Guide to Safely and Confidently Navigate Water, Weather, and Winds

SBN: 978-1-56523-554-0
$19.95 • 160 Pages

Boat Maintenance
The Complete Guide to Keeping Your Boat Shipshape

ISBN: 978-1-56523-549-6
$19.95 • 160 Pages

Boating Disasters
How to Avoid, and Survive, the Most Common to Extreme Mishaps on the Water

ISBN: 978-1-56523-590-8
$14.95 • 160 Pages